YOUR PASSPORT TO

CHINA

Douglas Hustad

raintree
a Capstone company — publishers for children

Raintree is an imprint of Capstone Global Library Limited, a company incorporated in England and Wales having its registered office at 264 Banbury Road, Oxford, OX2 7DY – Registered company number: 6695582

www.raintree.co.uk
myorders@raintree.co.uk

Edited by Jamie Hudalla
Designed by Colleen McLaren
Original illustrations © Capstone Global Library Limited 2021
Originated by Capstone Global Library Ltd
Printed and bound in India

978 1 3982 0543 7 (hardback)
978 1 3982 0544 4 (paperback)

British Library Cataloguing in Publication Data
A full catalogue record for this book is available from the British Library.

Acknowledgements
We would like to thank the following for permission to reproduce photographs: Red Line Editorial: 5; Shutterstock Images: Aquarius Studio, 24, aquatarkus, 11, Artsem Vysotski, cover (flag), Asia Images Group, 22, dangdumrong, 18, Dmitry Chulov, 29, Dmitry Kalinovsky, 7, Eugene Ga, 27, Hung Chung Chih, 6, Jo Panuwat D, 16, Joshua Davenport, 17, Meiqianbao, 9, Sihasakprachum, 14, SL-Photography, 21, T. Lesia, cover (map), Yuri Yavnik, 13, zhao jiankang, cover (bottom)
Design Elements: iStockphoto, Shutterstock Images

We would like to thank Hai Ren, Associate Professor at the East Asian Studies and Anthropology Department of the University of Arizona, USA, for his assistance in the preparation of this book.

CONTENTS

Words in **bold** are in the glossary.

CHAPTER ONE

WELCOME TO CHINA!

A tall gate looms over the Forbidden City. Hundreds of buildings and palaces are nestled within the gated area. It is in Beijing, China's capital. About 16 million people visit the Forbidden City every year. But before 1912, ordinary people couldn't get close to it. It was the home of Chinese rulers for 500 years. Only the ruling class was allowed in. Today, tourists visit it from other countries. They pass through the gate that was once only used for rulers.

China's past can be seen alongside its present. Just a few kilometres away from the Forbidden City is the Beijing National Stadium. This stadium was built to host the 2008 Olympic Games. It is also hosting the 2022 Winter Olympics. The stadium combines new technology with ancient traditions. The twisted steel makes a pattern typical of the designs of Chinese **ceramics**.

MAP OF CHINA

Great Wall of China ▲

CHINA

BEIJING ■

Terracotta
Warriors of Xian ◆

Beijing
National
Stadium ▲

★ Wolong National
Nature Reserve

● Lijiang

Tian Tan
Buddha

Hong
Kong ● ◆

Key:
■ Capital City
● City
▲ Landmark
★ Park
◆ Attraction

N
W ✦ E
S

Explore China's cities
and landmarks.

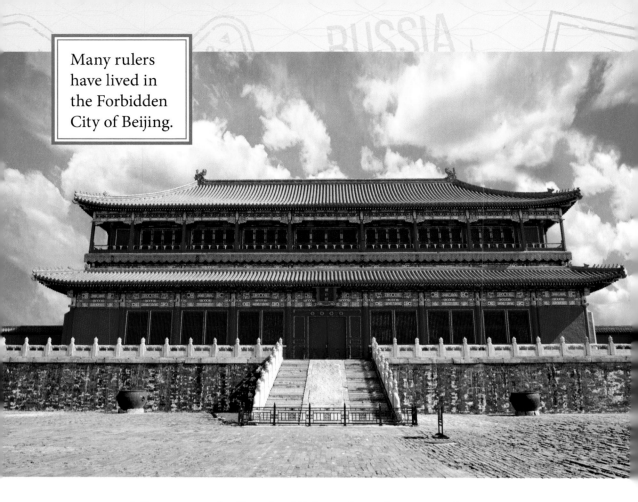

Many rulers have lived in the Forbidden City of Beijing.

More people live in China than in any other country. China is also the second-largest country in the world in terms of land. It shares borders with 14 countries. These include Russia, India and North Korea. More than 90 per cent of China's population is Han Chinese. They are the world's largest **ethnic group**. The Han have lived in China for thousands of years. There are also 55 other recognized ethnic groups in China.

The Yao people are one of 55 recognized ethnic groups in China.

FACT FILE

OFFICIAL NAME: PEOPLE'S REPUBLIC OF CHINA
POPULATION: 1.4 BILLION
LAND AREA: 9.3 MILLION SQ .KM (3.6 MILLION SQ. MI)
CAPITAL: BEIJING
MONEY: RENMINBI OR YUAN
GOVERNMENT: AUTHORITARIAN STATE
LANGUAGE: MANDARIN CHINESE OR STANDARD CHINESE
GEOGRAPHY: Located in East Asia, China shares long land borders with Mongolia, Russia and India. Many other countries, including Vietnam, Myanmar and Kazakhstan, also border China. The East China Sea borders a portion of the country too.
NATURAL RESOURCES: China has coal, iron ore, rice, soya beans, oil and natural gas.

CHAPTER TWO

HISTORY OF CHINA

The rulers of the Shang Dynasty were the first recorded rulers of China. A dynasty is a family of rulers. The Shang ruled 3,600 years ago. That was around 1600 **BCE**. China was not a unified country yet. It was made up of territories. The territories fought with each other. In 221 BCE, the Qin Dynasty took over six territories held by the Zhou Dynasty. That gave the Qin control over the country. The Qin started the first empire in China. Qin Shi Huang was the first **emperor**.

INVENTIONS

China has made some of the world's greatest inventions. Paper was invented in China in the 100s **CE**. The Chinese invented gunpowder and the printing press in the 800s. The first printed book was made in 868. China **exported** its goods throughout the world. Chinese silk and pottery were first sold in Europe in the 1500s.

Many **artefacts** have been recovered from the Shang Dynasty.

CHINA'S DYNASTIES

1600-1050 BCE: Shang
1046-256 BCE: Zhou
221-206 BCE: Qin
206 BCE-220 CE: Han
220-265: Three Kingdoms
of Cao Wei, Shu Han and
Dong Wu
265-420: Jin
386-589: Period of Northern
and Southern Dynasties

581-618: Sui
618-906: Tang
907-960: Five Dynasties Period
960-1279: Song
1279-1368: Yuan
1368-1644: Ming
1644-1911: Qing

THE END OF DYNASTIES

A series of dynasties controlled China for thousands of years. Dynasties often fought each other for power. The country went through many changes. Through wars, China's borders moved in and out. The last ruling dynasty was the Qing Dynasty. It ended in 1911. At the time there had been several disasters with the **economy**. The Chinese people overthrew the Qing Dynasty. They formed a **republic** in 1912. But not everyone agreed with the new government. Two groups battled for control. The Nationalist Party took control.

A statue of Mao Zedong was erected in Lijiang.

Then the Communist Party formed in 1921. The two parties fought during the Japanese invasion of China (1937–1945). They still fought during the Chinese Civil War (1945–1949). The Communist Party won in 1949. It formed the People's Republic of China. The party leader was Mao Zedong. He became the new leader of China.

CHINA TODAY

The Communist Party of China is an authoritarian power today. This means it has control over the people. The leader of the party is also the president of the country. Xi Jinping was elected president in 2013. As of 2018, China no longer limits how long someone can be president.

CHAPTER THREE

EXPLORE CHINA

The Great Wall of China winds thousands of kilometres through the countryside. The Chinese built the first sections of the wall more than 2,500 years ago. They built it for protection against **invaders** from the north. The wall has protected China from many enemies. Its total length increased to 21,196 kilometres (13,170 miles). If the wall were straight, it could stretch more than halfway around the Earth!

FACT

The Great Wall of China is the longest wall ever built.

Chinese workers built the wall by hand. Its bricks are made of soil and stone. The wall ranges from 5 to 9 metres (15 to 30 feet) high. Some parts of the wall have collapsed over the years.

The Great Wall of China protected China from many invaders.

Visitors to Xian can see where the Terracotta Warriors were unearthed.

One section of the wall was rebuilt in the 1950s. It is close to Beijing. Many tourists visit it. About 10 million people visit this section of wall each year.

THE TERRACOTTA WARRIORS OF XIAN

One of history's greatest discoveries started with digging a well. In 1974, a Chinese farmer hit something solid with his shovel. This revealed an army of statues. They were made of terracotta, a type of clay. More digging revealed thousands of statues. They are known as the Terracotta Warriors of Xian.

They represent the army of China's first emperor. His subjects made the terracotta army when he died in 210 BCE. They believed the clay soldiers would protect the emperor in his afterlife.

The statues are near Xian in central China. The emperor is also buried near by. Not all the warriors have been uncovered yet. Experts estimate there are more than 8,000! One million people go to see the warriors each year.

People can ride in cable cars to reach the Tian Tan Buddha.

BIG BUDDHA

Tian Tan Buddha is a statue on Lantau Island. The island is part of Hong Kong. The statue is commonly called the Big Buddha. It stands 34 metres (112 feet) high. Visitors climb 268 steps to reach the base of the statue.

Buddha was the founder of the religion of Buddhism. The statue shows Buddha sitting and holding up his right hand. This is a gesture of blessing. The statue was finished in 1993. Tourists can walk up to the Buddha. They must pay to go inside. Legend says that some of Buddha's ashes are in there.

It took 12 years to build the Tian Tan Buddha.

Pandas eat a lot of bamboo!

PANDAS

The giant panda is one of the national symbols of China. These bears only live in a few mountain ranges in south-western China. They used to be much more common. But hunting and the destruction of forests have lowered their numbers. There are now fewer than 2,000 pandas in the wild.

Visitors can still see the pandas. The Wolong National Nature Reserve is near the pandas' natural **habitat**. Researchers care for the bears there. At Dujiangyan Panda Base, visitors learn about the effort to save pandas. They can see the bears up-close.

FACT

A giant panda eats mostly bamboo. Pandas eat 9–18 kilograms (20–40 pounds) of it each day.

CHAPTER FOUR

DAILY LIFE

China has more than 15 megacities. A megacity has more than 10 million people. Many people work 8 to 12 hours a day in these cities. The electronics industry is growing in China. There are many opportunities for work. That is why so many people move to cities.

RURAL LIFE

More than 500 million people still live in rural countryside areas. Many of them are farmers. Some travel to China's growing cities. They work in construction and business for a while. Then they move back to the country. Life in the country is different from that in cities. Many people still live in wooden houses. Some cook over an open fire. People have fewer job opportunities. They generally have less money.

Some people in rural China grow rice in rice fields.

Many Chinese people value family relationships.

RELIGION AND FAMILY

China officially recognizes four religions. These religions are Taoism, Buddhism, Islam and Christianity. Chinese people historically practised Buddhism, Taoism and Confucianism. These are known as the three teachings. These traditions are still present in Chinese culture.

Many Chinese people also care about honouring their **ancestors**. They have respect for family. These values come from Confucianism. Followers believe that relationships with family are the most important relationships in a person's life. Children are expected to care for their elderly parents.

FACT
China is home to the greatest number of cyclists in the world. There are about half a billion bicycles in China. Many people cycle to work.

Chinese people use chopsticks to eat.

CULTURAL CUISINE

Families often share big meals together. But China is a huge country. Typical meals can vary. Many Chinese people in the southern provinces meet with friends and family for dim sum. Dim sum is a meal with small plates of foods such as dumplings. The foods are shared around the table.

Chinese people often drink tea with a meal. A traditional Chinese table is made of wood or bamboo. People sit on bamboo mats or on small wooden chairs. The food is placed in the centre. People pass dishes round and take the food with chopsticks.

Rice is served at almost at every meal. It is considered polite to fill the rice bowls for older people out of respect.

Dinner is the biggest meal of the day. Chinese people enjoy many types of food. The people of the south-western Sichuan province enjoy spicy food. In the winter, people across the country enjoy heating a hotpot. It is like a soup. They cook foods such as meat in it.

SESAME PEANUT BUTTER NOODLES

These noodles are a version of Chinese sesame noodles. Noodles are combined with a simple sauce for a tasty dish. With the help of an adult, you can make this meal at home.

Ingredients:

- 170 grams soba noodles
- 2 tablespoons sesame oil
- 1 ½ tablespoons peanut butter
- 2 tablespoons honey
- 2 tablespoons soy sauce
- 1 ½ tablespoons rice vinegar
- 1 clove of minced garlic
- ½ teaspoon of grated ginger

Method:

1. Cook the noodles in boiling water.
2. In a bowl, mix together the sesame oil, peanut butter, honey, soy sauce, rice vinegar, garlic and ginger. The sauce should be mixed until smooth.
3. When the noodles are ready, drain and combine with the sauce.

CHAPTER FIVE

HOLIDAYS AND CELEBRATIONS

Chinese New Year is the biggest holiday in China. China used to follow a different calendar from the rest of the world. Most of China's holidays still follow the old calendar. Chinese New Year takes place in January or February. It is also known as the Spring Festival. Families and friends get together to celebrate. They feast on treats such as dumplings and spring rolls.

NATIONAL DAY

China celebrates National Day on the 1st of October. That was the date the People's Republic formed in 1949. The country celebrates with festivals and parades. The biggest parade happens in Beijing. The military marches, and tanks follow. The president makes an appearance. The whole celebration ends with fireworks over the Forbidden City.

People light lanterns to symbolise the start of a new year.

New Year is a time of fresh starts. People clean out their homes. They get rid of things they don't need. They believe this washes away the bad luck of the old year.

COLOURFUL FESTIVALS

The Lantern Festival comes at the end of the New Year celebrations. People light lanterns. This symbolises a new start in the New Year. The Dragon Boat Festival is in summer. It celebrates the fifth month of China's old calendar. People build and race boats with a dragon's head at the front.

CHAPTER SIX

SPORT AND RECREATION

China has a long history of making art. The Chinese invented bronze 5,000 years ago. They have been making teapots, cups and more out of this metal ever since.

GO

Go is a Chinese board game. It is one of the oldest games in the world. Two people play the game. It is usually played with a Go game board and playing pieces of two different colours, called stones.

1. Each player picks one colour of stone.
2. Each player takes turns placing their stones on a board. Stones cannot be moved once they are placed.
3. Each player tries to capture the other player's stone by fully surrounding it with their own stones.
4. The game continues until both players are unable to make a move.

People practise tai chi to feel at peace.

The Chinese also make kites and lanterns out of paper. Kites are made to look beautiful in flight. Lanterns are used in China's holidays and festivals.

SUCCESS IN SPORT

Sport has also been important in China since ancient times. Tai chi is a kind of **martial art**. It involves making specific movements that are calming and peaceful. China has become a world sport destination since it hosted the 2008 Summer Olympics. Sport, historical sites and rich culture are all great reasons for people to visit China.

GLOSSARY

ancestor
family member who lived a long time ago

artefact
human-made object, usually of historical interest

BCE/CE
BCE means Before Common Era, or before year one. CE means Common Era, or after year one.

ceramics
objects such as bowls and vases that are made from clay

economy
wealth and resources in a country

emperor
male ruler of an area or country

ethnic group
people who share a common culture, race, language or nationality

export
sell and ship products to other countries

habitat
environment in which an animal or plant lives

invaders
people who enter other areas and take control of them

martial art
ancient Chinese style of fighting or self-defence

republic
type of government where people elect their political leaders and president

FIND OUT MORE

BOOKS

All About China: Stories, Songs, Crafts and Games for Kids, Allison Branscombe (Tuttle Publishing, 2018)

Following the Great Wall (Unfolding Journeys) Stewart Ross (Lonely Planet Kids, 2017)

Let's Cook!: The Culture and Recipes of China, Tracey Kelly (Raintree, 2020)

WEBSITES

www.dkfindout.com/uk/history/ancient-china
DKfindout! gives you fun facts about ancient China.

www.kids-world-travel-guide.com/china-facts.html
This Travel Guide website tells you lots of interesting information about China.

www.natgeokids.com/uk/discover/geography/countries/30-cool-facts-about-china
Find out some cool facts about China with National Geographic.

INDEX

OTHER BOOKS IN THIS SERIES

YOUR PASSPORT TO ECUADOR

YOUR PASSPORT TO EL SALVADOR

YOUR PASSPORT TO ETHIOPIA

YOUR PASSPORT TO FRANCE

YOUR PASSPORT TO IRAN

YOUR PASSPORT TO KENYA

YOUR PASSPORT TO PERU

YOUR PASSPORT TO RUSSIA

YOUR PASSPORT TO SPAIN